CHAPTER 1
THE TRADITIONAL FORMULA

The Largest American Lie

Learn the Truth

Most people, from the time of their early childhood up through what they are taught in school and continuing through early adulthood, have been taught there is a specific formula that is to be followed by anyone who wishes to have a successful life, career, and retirement. Anyone who does not abide by these standards, is said to be doomed to a life of mediocrity and insignificance.

Like a fine holiday tradition, this traditional "path to success" is passed down from generation to generation. It is expected to be upheld in full in all of its entirety and then passed down to the next generation as the cycle repeats. In some countries outside of America, families take this formula so seriously, that if their children were to stray, they would consider going as far as disowning them from the family.

Anyone that wishes to avoid tragedy and poverty must follow these simple steps or forever be associated with the underachievers. These steps are quite simple for most people. In fact, they are ingrained into our minds from an early age, but it does not stop there. As we progress throughout our lives, this formula is only taken more seriously, and is an absolute must to prevent our lives from taking the ultimate downward spiral. This path is completed by following these 6 steps:

    1) Go to school. Get good grades, and graduate high school. If you are highly successful in high school, you may even receive scholarships and/or grants to help you throughout the next step.

    2) Once you are out of high school, you must select a career and pick a college that helps you master the skills necessary in the particular field you have chosen. If you are lucky, you may have get

assistance in paying your way through school. However, sadly, a large majority of kids are not so fortunate.

3) Once you have graduated with your college education, it is now time to move **forward and pursue your selected career.** The time has come to complete a detailed resume, submit it to any person of interest in your chosen field who will possibly look at it, and become what you spent all those long hours, courses, and years studying to become. Your goals and aspirations are finally in sight, as you start to see everything you have worked for come together.

4) Now that you have landed your "dream job", it is now time to show your value to your company. Most of us are told, that if we work hard, follow instructions, take little time off, and do more than what we are paid to do, we will have the opportunity to move up in the company. This will bring with it increased

salary, increased benefits and possibly more vacation time. We are taught that if you remain loyal to your company of choice, they will remain loyal to you, as you will help one another prosper for years to come.

5) If you are lucky, you will climb our corporate ladder quickly and efficiently, and you will be rewarded for your efforts with a generous retirement plan after many years of hard work. For most people, this process will easily stretch into their golden years before it is completed.

6) Your efforts and loyalty to your company have paid off! Now you are able to enjoy the final years of your life with being financially comfortable, as well as having the time freedom to participate in the activities you enjoy most.

Sounds fair enough does it not? These six steps have been carried out by our parents before us and by their parents before them. Typically, if one was to go in a different direction than what has been described, they would be frowned upon by their family, mocked by their peers, and labeled by society as an individual that has no brighter future than that of a burger flipper at McDonalds. Given these circumstances, few have been willing to select a different path...... *until now.*

CHAPTER 2
HOLES IN THE FORMULA

The Largest American Lie

Learn the Truth

 The traditional formula to the road of success sounds pretty spectacular, does it not? Most individuals find it safe and promising. Unfortunately, this is not always the case. A majority of people do have bumps along the way that are never anticipated. History has begun to teach us of our errors in judgement. Increasingly, more people have started to take notice of some of the gaping holes that can easily and unexpectedly come with relying primarily on this train of thought.
 The first problem with this line of thinking is for a majority of college kids who are not lucky enough to receive assistance in paying for their

college education. This becomes a very real dilemma for a large number of college graduates, as they find themselves having to pay back a mountain of debt right out of college that, more often than not, seems insurmountable. We are at a time in our economy in which student loan debts are at an all-time high, and many college graduates underestimate the challenges of starting off their adult life with such a heavy burden of debt. This will be touched upon further in Chapter 3.

Problem number two lies in the situation they find themselves after their graduation ceremony has concluded and they set out to find their "dream job". They create their resume, start the job search, and run into possibly the most common problem that is experienced.... They cannot find a job! In our current day society, college graduates are starting to find that employers are beginning to value experience more than any other qualification found on a resume. Most college graduates have many things going for them, but typically experience is the one thing they lack most. This puts many individuals in a tight bind.

    The next flaw we see with the traditional formula is best illustrated in a common placed scenario. Picture in this example, that our bright faced achiever does in fact land the job he has been wanting. He is finally employed in his preferred field and enjoying the work that he carries out. However, he soon realizes that he is in fact working for a boss that dislikes him, overlooks him, or finds him a threat to his own position with the company. To completely understand this gaping hole, one must understand that bosses are no different from the employees in many aspects. They also have a boss to whom they must answer, and despite the misconception that the company remains loyal to the workers, they can at times see a bright faced college graduate with a world of ability, as a threat to their position with the company. They then have the fear that the new employee will sooner or later be a substantial threat to their own job. To protect their own interests, they will undermine, overlook, and possibly purposely ignore their achievements. Some individuals face this particular challenge throughout their entire career with the company, leaving them no room to climb the corporate ladder, despite their excellent performance.

Let's imagine for a moment that someone successfully avoids all of these potential disasters and lands the job they desire with a boss that values them. All is right with the world.... Until the company they are working for either goes out of business, putting a large number of employees out of work, or even merges together with another company in their industry, causing the newly combined company to not have need for as many workers. This in turn causes the newly formed company to make massive layoffs of workers and possibly even entire departments.

I would say the most tragic and most likely bump in the road is met at the end of the journey, when the time for retirement has arrived. All of your years of blood, sweat, and tears are finally supposed to pay off at the finish line..... until you discover that well into your 60s you do not have enough money saved up to hang up your jersey just yet. You are then forced to continue working well into your golden years with no potential end in sight. Sad to say, in today's day of the 21st century, this is more common than it ever has been before due to our suffering economy and workers being underpaid.

We live in a new age. It is starting to become more and more apparent that the common, normal way of finding success that has been crammed down our throats since birth, will not reward us like we are promised it will - not in the world we live in today. More frequently than ever, people are finding that the common methods are no longer the slam dunk we have been brought up believing them to be. We are increasingly seeing people take different paths of their own to find success in ways that were not thought possible 30 years ago.

My problem with the traditional formula is actually much simpler than some of these scenarios. I have watched and observed for years the traditional formula at work in people's lives, and I have come to a conclusion about three glaring personal issues that I do not desire for myself:

1) I do not believe we as human beings should be told by someone else our worth in the form of a dollar amount by another human being. I am a firm believer that each of us has unlimited potential, and that we should be the sole decision makers in not only our line of work, but also in the amount of monetary value we are able to achieve. Our destinies should be determined by our own hands. A majority of the bumps in the road that were described left us with no control over the situation.

2) Call me crazy, but I believe that no person should have the authority to be placed above us. We should be the ones that determine when we show up to work, when we take our lunch break,

when we are allowed to go to the bathroom, and when we can go home after a hard day's work.
3) My final issue with this thought process, is that most people do not aim for a life above average. In a culture where most people follow one path to success, we must find an alternative road of our own if we wish to stand out. As the saying goes, if you wish to have a life greater than that of an ordinary person, you must not pursue the path of the average.

Now before anyone that has read up until this point starts thinking thoughts such as, "Well my parents went to college, and they turned out pretty good!", I must warn you to not take what I am saying out of context. For a significant number of people, a college education is the correct path to go. Individuals that seek careers such as doctors and lawyers, have chosen a path in which a degree is 100% required in their line of work. A small minority of success chasers will find success with the traditional formula. However, for a large number of people, another method is needed.

It is a new world we now live in. Government policies have drastically changed. Our economy has drastically changed. Our society has drastically changed. The time has come for an alternative path to success to emerge as a result. This, is the day of the entrepreneur.

CHAPTER 3
THE FACTS

The Largest American Lie

Learn the Truth

Let me paint a picture for you. We have a young man.... We will call him Mike. Mike is a young, 20-year-old kid, with an unlimited amount of ability and promise. He is interested in a career in psychology because he is told by a friend it pays well. He enrolls in a well-respected college, with a strong program in the subject. The first step in that specific field is to get a Bachelor's degree, which takes a minimum of 4 years, so Mike does this. He works hard, stays out of trouble, and earns his degree in the 4-year period. Mike decides then to continue forward to get his Master's Degree in the field, which takes him an additional 3 years. By the end of the process, Mike has spent a total of 7 years getting his degree.

Mike is now 27 years old. His student loan debt has totaled over $80,000, causing him to have to make payments in the ball park of $800 monthly. At that rate, it would take him around 10 years to pay it off completely. Straight out of college, Mike is unable to get the job he pictured right at first, so he settles for a job as a high school psychologist, which pays him $70,000 a year. Mike's salary is decent, but the student loan debt, combined with typical monthly bills, such as rent, car payment, car insurance, etc., make him just able to squeeze by financially, but he survives.

Two years later, the school board decides to make cuts, and they decide that Mike is expendable. Mike now sees himself drowning in debt, led by his student loan debt. He is unable to find work in his field so he takes a job that is not related to his degree. His income goes from $70,000 down to just under $40,000 almost overnight. Mike files for bankruptcy, which helps with his other forms of debt but does nothing to help his student loan debt, which remains. Mike is now over 29 years old, and finds his life has no direction, and his student loan is not going anywhere.

If you think that Mike's unfortunate story is "just a story", you may find it is not as farfetched as you may think. College graduates are beginning to find that pursuing a college degree comes with more challenges than ever before. The payoff that is promised with these challenges is less likely to bear fruit than any other time in our history, making it a rather risky investment.

Let us begin with looking at some of the statistics found with student loan debts in 2016 going forward. The average college debt for graduates in 2016 is over $37,000. That is 6% higher number than it was in 2015. College graduates are finding that they are facing higher student loan debts than any period in our lifetime! 43 million Americans are victims of student loan debt. The national student loan debt as I write this is over 1 trillion dollars.

I know what you are thinking, "We may have debt, but at least we will be well equipped to find high paying jobs to deal with this debt thanks to our college educations!". Unfortunately, not so much. It is increasingly becoming more documented on how unlikely a college degree really is to land you that perfect job in the 21st century. In 2013, the Washington Post published an article on the very topic. It stated that only around 27% of college graduates end up working in the field they majored in. In 2015, Time Magazine published an article, that stated 49% of college graduates were either underemployed, or were working at a job that does not require a college degree at all. With the odds of landing even a decent job being the same odds as that of accurately guessing the correct results of a coin flip, this makes the student loan national average of $37,000 a frightening investment to say the least.

More and more kids put themselves in financial turmoil, with a 50/50 shot at even getting the job they work so hard to acquire.

Another alarming fact is that student loan debt is the only type of debt that cannot be helped by filing for bankruptcy. This makes it a tight squeeze to get out of for those 49% of college graduates that are underemployed, who are living pay check to paycheck just to pay their monthly expenses.

The time for change is now. The time to be outstanding is at our door step. The only solution to these gaping holes in the traditional system we have all been convinced that will provide for us, is to find a more efficient and modern way to find success. The traditional formula we have all been fed since our childhoods is outdated for many of us. It no longer holds any relevancy for a large portion of the population. As I stated before, some individuals will find the success they are looking for by following the traditional formula, but it is at a smaller minority than ever before.

Your friends, family, and possibly even loved ones will not understand, nor support your decision to seek other possibilities. Every great person throughout history made some decisions early on in their journeys for which they were ridiculed, and shamed. Regardless, those decisions turned out to be remembered as brilliant.

It has been commonly perceived that the only way to find success in this life without following the typical path was to do something near to impossible, such as becoming a professional athlete, a famous musician, a film star, or some other type of celebrity. The chances of something like that taking place is normally slim to none. We have a better way.

CHAPTER 4
WHAT CAN WE DO?

The Largest American Lie

Learn the Truth

As stated prior, the traditional way of thinking does work for some people. It is important to comprehend that going to college, getting a job where you truly have no power, and hoping that company will take care of you into retirement is NOT the scam here. They are reputable choices that do have some possibility of bringing in some pay off. Some instances, do in fact turn out just as the step by step description in Chapter 1 portrayed it. As previously stated, some careers require that you have a degree in the certain field to even have a chance of sniffing a job (such as doctors or lawyers being two examples.)

That part of the equation is not the scam here. What is the scam in all of this is the common notion that many of us grew up with...... that it is either the traditional way or bust. It was that college was an absolute must. A large majority of Americans have been brainwashed into thinking there is only one reputable way. It is programmed into our heads by our parents, by our schools early on, and continues into college, right into our careers. It is a never ending cycle of ignorance.

It used to be in many areas of the country (and even the world), that if you opposed the "right way" to find success, it was an unheard of offense. You may as well be preparing yourself to get stoned by your peers, metaphorically speaking.

This is the time of the entrepreneur. Many people never consider it, but becoming an entrepreneur is the perfect way of taking life like a bull by the horns, and channeling it in any direction you so please. Did you ever think to yourself up until this far that perhaps I could be my own boss? That just maybe, I can be the one that determines my income, how much and when I work, and even what type of work I am going to do? "Sounds too good to be true," You may be thinking.

It is not. I am not claiming that all entrepreneurs don't go to college. I am simply stating that history has taught us that a degree is not necessary (which we will discuss further in Chapter 5). Entrepreneurs work hard, have difficulty seeing things the way they normally are, and are not easily excited about following rules. If you enjoy being lazy (and do not wish to change that trait), and are quite fond of the rules and barriers placed around you, then this book, simply put, is not for you.

In order to better understand the term entrepreneur, let us look at the dictionary definition of the word itself: "a person who organizes and operates a business or businesses, taking on greater than normal financial risk in order to do so." Fairly simple enough wouldn't you agree? When most see the phrase "greater than normal financial risk", they automatically assume they are going to have to pour out their life savings and be in debt forever. Let's not make it so dramatic. Keep in mind what monetary risk the average person puts toward their jobs. Really think about it. It normally is not much. Perhaps a new pair of shoes every once in a while, or possibly even a new suit here and there if they have a high up corporate position, the point being made, that greater than normal does not always have to be a very large amount.

A greater than normal money investment could be $100, $1,000, or even $10,000. Mainly it is dependent on what type of business you want to establish. The way I see, it there are five types of entrepreneurs:

1) The Traditional: This type of business owner takes everything they have, and goes for broke. They build a business on their backs. They work long hours, manage the business themselves, and some may look at them as letting their business run them instead of the

other way around. Normally, in this instance, the type of business the owner runs could be a restaurant, possibly an automobile shop, or maybe even a small grocery store. The money that it takes to start this type of business is similar to what the average student loan debt is currently, likely north of $30,000. It could be higher, and it could be lower. It is simply dependent on what type of business you wish to run.

2) The Creator: In my opinion, this type of entrepreneur may possibly be one of the most difficult types to become. That being said, it takes place successfully more than we realize. The creator is something that simply creates a type of product or service, that does not yet exist. Think Mark Zuckerberg with Facebook. Many people have great ideas, but do not pursue them. The individuals that act on their inventive ideas are the ones that become highly successful entrepreneurs.

3) The High Bidder: The High Bidder is someone that already has a fairly substantial amount of wealth and success, who purchases out smaller businesses. Some examples of this that you may know of might be Warren Buffet or Donald Trump.

4) The Landlord: Pretty self-explanatory is it not? The landlord owns something extra that they do not need themselves, so they rent it out to someone else to make a profit. Typically, this is most commonly done by renting out houses. Some landlords think even bigger and rent out apartments. This does not always have to be done with a form of real estate. It could be done with automobiles, clothing, or even household supplies amongst others.

5) The Half Breed: This is perhaps the most controversial type of business owner. The Half Breed, is someone who is indeed self-employed, but is not the

owner or creator of the products they market. Examples of this might be a self-employed independent insurance agent, Real Estate agent, Stock broker, or Network Marketer. What do all of these have in common? They all distribute a service for one/multiple companies in a certain industry. It has been debated for a long stretch of time whether these types of individuals are considered true entrepreneurs. From my perspective, I say that they do belong on this list. They have no boss, answer to themselves, decide when they work and do not work, and have no limit to the amount of income they can earn. However, the products they are distributing are not their own products, so we will say they are Half Breed entrepreneurs.

If you carefully examine each of these options of entrepreneurship, it can be found that each one holds hundreds of different options within them. Every type of business that was discussed have multiple different types of businesses that fall into each category. This can truly make the possibilities for any soon to be entrepreneur endless!

    Some roads to entrepreneurship cost thousands of dollars of startup fees. Others can be started with a few hundred dollars. How big a person wants to build is dependent on their individual drive, motivation, confidence, and vision. What is so beloved about this path, is anything you wish to be, anything you wish to accomplish, you CAN do it. No one is sabotaging your success and progress, and the results you see at the end of the journey are on your shoulders, no one else's.

    When comparing the path of an entrepreneur, to the traditional path, our formula has more upside and potential. If you gather anything from this book, I would like it to be these 3 points.

1) Experience always trumps degrees.
2) The faster you fail, the faster you learn.

3) Self-education will always beat out classroom education.

We will discuss these three statements in detail in the chapters to come. As I stated earlier, your friends, peers, and loved ones will not understand your journey. Every person that ever did something significant throughout history developed hate, criticism, and skeptics. Crowds of people will call you crazy. Close to no one will believe in you.... that is until you become successful. Then everyone will want to know your secrets and how you did it. I will end this chapter with a quote from the great Steve Jobs, founder of Apple Inc.

"Here's to the crazy ones, the misfits, the rebels, the troublemakers, the round pegs in the square holes.... The ones who see things differently. They're not fond of rules... You can quote them, disagree with them, glorify or vilify them, but the only thing you can't do is ignore them because they change things.... They push the human race forward, and while some may see them as the crazy ones, we see genius, because the ones who are crazy enough to think they can change the world are the ones who do." -Steven Paul Jobs

CHAPTER 5
HISTORY SPEAKS

The Largest American Lie

Learn the Truth

Self-education will always beat out classroom education.... This can be supported through examples throughout history in the business world. There have been literally hundreds of different instances where some of the biggest names in the business world did things society would say, "cannot be done", without a college education.

In 1972, a company by the name of Unadultered Food Products was founded by 3 men in Long Island New York. The company originally was created to provide fruit juices to a variety of health and wellness locations. The small company was one of the first juice companies of its time to use natural ingredients. Hyman Golden, one of the three founders of the company and chairmen of the board for a number of years, did not even complete high school. In the 1980s, the company changed its name to Snapple, and today the company is one of the largest beverage supplying companies in the world. A lack of a degree did not hold back Hyman Golden from assisting in founding the company, as well as serving as its chairman for a number of years. In Golden's case, he did not even complete high school.

Have you ever heard of a company called Ford Automotive? I do hope so, because this company is one of the largest automotive providers in the world today. Not many people remember back to the days when the company was founded in 1903, by a man by the name of Henry Ford. Henry Ford was one of the first self-made billionaires, and is remembered today as an all-time great innovator and visionary. He was able to produce the first automobile that was affordable to the public. His work caused the company to soar into an industry leader, and is even a giant over a century later. Henry Ford did not attend any form of college.

One of my personal favorite stories, is that of one Bob Proctor. Bob is a high school and college drop out. At the age of 26, his life was looking to be going nowhere. A friend of Bob's gave him a book called, Think and Grow Rich (one of the top personal growth books that has ever been written) by Napoleon Hill. The very year he read that book, he started his own company that offered cleaning services. In less than a 12-month span, his company had expanded to multiple countries. Today, Bob Proctor is a successful author, motivational speaker, and business consultant. He has played a big role in the project of The Secret, which focuses on teaching the Law of Attraction, and is one of the most well respected names in business world and Network Marketing Industry.

A man by the name of Joyce C. Hall was a college no show at the age of 18. He started making and selling greeting cards in the early

1900's. He ended up creating a company called Hallmark Cards. As of 2014, the company was worth over 3 billion dollars and is the largest greeting card company in the world.

Andrew Carnegie was one of the pioneers of the steel industry in the 1800s. His fortune by the final years of his life was in the hundreds of millions of dollars. The final years of his life he chose to give away 90% of his money, which was over 350 million dollars. In 2015, that would be equivalent to over 78 billion dollars. He will forever be remembered as not only a great business man, but also as a great philanthropist. Andrew Carnegie was an elementary school dropout.

Richard Schulze, was the founder of the popular electronic store Best Buy. He was 25 years old when he founded what started as a small electrical store. As of 2015, his net worth is $2.6 Billion. Richard Schulze...... you guessed it, did not attend college.

We could literally go on forever when it comes to entrepreneurs throughout history that did not

attend college or dropped out before finishing. Other notable names include:
1) Steve Jobs: Co-founder of Apple Inc.
2) Richard Branson: Founder of multiple companies including Virgin Records, Virgin Atlantic Airways, and Virgin Mobile.
3) Richard DeVos: Co-founder of Amway.
4) Daniel Abraham: Founder of Slim-fast.
5) Steve Madden: Famous shoe designer.
6) Walt Disney: Founder of Walt Disney Inc.
7) Milton Hershey: Founder of Hershey's Milk Chocolate.
8) Mary Kay Ash: Founder of Mary Kay Inc.
9) John D. Rockefeller: Founder of Standard Oil.
10) Jack Crawford Taylor: Founder of Enterprise Rent-a-Car.
11) David Neeleman: Founder of Jet Blue.
12) David Oreck: Founder of The Oreck Corp.

13) Colonel Harlan Sanders: Founder of Kentucky Fried Chicken.
14) Michael Dell: Founder of Dell.
15) W. Clement Stone: Founder of Success Magazine.
16) Oprah Winfrey: Famous television personality and entrepreneur, actress, and author.
17) Mark Zuckerberg: Founder of Facebook.
18) Bill Gates: Founder of Microsoft.
19) Ellen DeGeneres: Famous television personality and author.
20) David Thomas: Founder of Wendy's.

    Quite the hall of fame, wouldn't you concur? There are hundreds of other examples we could look at beyond this bunch, but I think you are starting to get the idea.
    It is not always the college dropout, or high school drop out that discourages entrepreneurs from attending college. Famous CEO of several private companies, bestselling author, and one of

the country's most well-known success coaches Grant Cardone, did go to college when he was young and walked away with a degree in accounting. He regularly states that it is nothing more than a piece of paper, and that it has done nothing to help him in his business career. Over the years he has also stated on social media that he would "trade his college degree for the success of any of these that didn't graduate," posting the quote next to pictures of Bill Gates, Walt Disney, Oprah Winfrey, Steve Jobs, amongst others. Grant has a net worth in the hundreds of millions of dollars.

    It has been proven over and over again throughout history, that not only is the traditional formula not needed for the entrepreneur, it is sometimes even discouraged if you want to be great. There is no need to waste your time studying topics you will never use in the business world, when you can be currently working towards your dreams and aspirations. All of these great entrepreneurs took a different path. We have been told a lie since we were infants, not that college can make you successful- that isn't the scam here. The scam is that we are told it is a must if you don't want to live a life of mediocrity. When you dig deep enough, it can be uncovered, that we have all been deceived.

CHAPTER 6
THE VALUE OF THE HALF BREED

The Largest American Lie

Learn the Truth

You do not have to create a multibillion dollar company to be a successful entrepreneur. I have known many individuals who pursue careers as half breed entrepreneurs (keep in mind, we have already established that these individuals have their place in the entrepreneur circle). A successful real estate agent, or insurance agent, can easily make over $100,000 a year with the proper motivation. I have known others that make up to as much as $500,000 a year. What I absolutely adore about this field is that the income is your decision. How much do you want, and how hard are you willing to work for it? A fantastic example of success in the Real

Estate business in particular, would be well known sales trainer and motivational speaker Tom Hopkins. Today, Tom is one of the most famous and household names in the sales education industry. Many people forget that he started out as a Real Estate Agent at the age of 19. In his first 6 months in the business, he made $42 a month. His car broke down on him, and he was struggling to survive. What caused Tom to struggle so much early on? As Tom himself puts it, he was not that great of a salesman. He did not have a background in selling, and did not know anything about it at that young age. He started to work on himself, and learn the art of selling, for months. From that point forward, he became the number one Real estate agent in California. At the age of 27, Tom was a millionaire.

Tom Hopkins is a shining example to the Real Estate business, and even to the entire half-breed entrepreneur pool itself. He was not naturally gifted as a salesman, and only through hard work and dedication did he become what he became.

There is a common misconception when it comes to sales of all kinds, that you need to just be naturally gifted to be a successful sales person. Are some individuals gifted? Absolutely. Are some individuals not as gifted? Absolutely! Regardless of natural God given talent, hard work can beat out talent any day of the week! Tom Hopkins is a perfect example of this.

Making over a six figure income puts you in the top 25% of income earners in America. Another exciting half breed industry that one could align themselves with is Network Marketing. This industry, like any other half breed field, has unlimited income earning potential. Not only that, you ARE your own boss. Self-employed is something most Americans would kill for! The Network Marketing industry typically gets a bad reputation, and this is what keeps a large majority of prospective entrepreneurs away. Simply put, ignorance and lack of education on the subject is the reason for most of the criticism.

When you get around the Networking industry, you hear a few phrases tossed around quite a bit.

Phrases such as "scam", or "pyramid scheme", which I would like to touch upon briefly. A true pyramid scheme is a business model that trades money around with no physical product or service to offer. Just the trading of money. It may not seem like it at first, but there is a large difference between a Network Marketing company and a Pyramid Scheme.

If you are thinking of joining a Network Marketing company, make sure to do your research ahead of time to make sure you are getting involved with a credible company with legitimate products. Do not be too concerned however, as there are literally hundreds of Network Marketing companies that operate legally around the world. Otherwise they would be shut down, due to the fact that Pyramid schemes are illegal.

What I have always found fondness in when it comes to the Network Marketing industry, is that you surround yourself with like-minded, hungry, inspiring individuals.

We as humans are like sponges. We soak up all the energy and information taking place around us. You can never find a better quality of people to learn from, than you can in the Network Marketing industry. This industry is how I gained my start in the business world. It gave me the mindset necessary to become an entrepreneur myself. I also met my wife as a result of the industry, as well as some of my closest friends. Network Marketing can be one of the best places to start your entrepreneur journey. I believe you can gain more valuable knowledge about money and business working with a good Network Marketing company for a year than you can gain with a four-year college degree. The information and lessons you will learn in that year will be more valuable in the business world than almost any college degree.

   This brings us back to the concept: experience always trumps degrees. You can study out of a textbook until your face is blue, but nothing will teach you more until you have gained that valuable experience of trying to sell something. That valuable experience of attempting to build a Network Marketing business is priceless.

    For all of the negative perception of the Networking industry, it is actually one of the largest, most successful industries in all the business world. Examples can be found that highlight the true potential of this controversial field. One that comes to mind, is Organo Gold distributor Holton Buggs. In college he pursued an engineering degree, but after quickly discovering that the engineering industry would never pay him the income he desired to fund his preferred lifestyle and would never give him the time freedom he desired, he dropped out. Organo Gold as a company was founded in 2008. Holton himself joined the company the same year, but had failed to be one the first enrollees. Such is a common myth that it is the only way to make it big in that type of company. By the time Holton joined the company, it had already amassed over 7,000 distributors. Through hard work and determination, he became at one time the top earner in all of the industry. In 2013, it surfaced that Holton was making an income of 1.3 million dollars per month (making his income over 15 million for the year).

If you have been around the Networking industry for any part of your life, you may have heard of a man by the name of Jim Rohn. Jim Rohn was a successful motivational speaker, author, and entrepreneur. Part of the reason he was (and still is) so wildly successful in the field of Network Marketing, is that he got his start as a tremendously successful Networker in his mid-20s. Rohn, openly and often, stated that it was not until the age of 25 that he became rich.

At the age of 25, he joined a direct selling company and was mentored by one of the founders of the company by the name of John Earl Shoaff. Shoaff introduced Rohn to the idea of personal development. The idea behind it all was that if you are willing to grow and develop your skills and who you are as a person, you will have a much easier time finding success because you have made yourself a much more capable person. Clearly it worked for Rohn. The way he explained it in many of his seminars was that from the age of 19 up through the age of 25, he was a poor man. From that time of 25 years of age up into his early 30s, he was a millionaire.

Jim Rohn is such a popular figure in the Network Marketing world, because not only is he a tremendous success story, but he was an avid supporter of the industry even after he moved on to other forms of business. He was a supporter, teacher, and inspiration to any Networker, and he was unapologetic about it.

The Value of the half-breed entrepreneur, regardless of what form he/she may come in, is extremely valuable to the business world. They remind everyone that no matter where you come from or what level of education you may carry under your belt, any one is capable of creating as high an income as they desire. Whether you seek a few 100,000 dollars a year or even a couple million, it is possible if your drive and work ethic match your goals.

One thing all half-breed's have in common, is they are all distributors in some way, shape, or form. They always act as a bridge between a company and the consumer, to deliver said company's product or service. The product or service does not belong to the distributor, and they do not make any decisions involving compensation, rules that are placed over them by the company, or even product changes in the marketplace. Because of this fact, this is why distributors of all forms are known as half-breed entrepreneurs. They relinquish a certain level of control in many important areas. However, they do keep control in regards to how much money they make (due to their production), how much (or how little) they choose to work, or even what company/companies they choose to distribute for if the relationship should sour for any particular reason. At the end of the day, they work for one person, the guy or gal looking back at them in the mirror. This makes them an entrepreneur by nature.

CHAPTER 7
DEFINE WHAT YOU WANT

The Largest American Lie

Learn the Truth

What is it that you wish to accomplish? Do you want to be self-sufficient and nothing more? Do you wish to simply get out of the job you hate? Could it be you desire to go down in history as a great individual? All of the above, and so much more are possible, as long as you believe you are capable of the task. Self-belief is one of the most powerful forces known to man. Nothing great ever accomplished was done without tremendous confidence and swagger. Don't believe me? Think of someone that you know (and we all know someone), who has absolutely no faith in themselves. Many of these individuals are good people with greatness in them. Everyone knows it, except for them, and if they do not see their own potential, that ability is not going to blossom.

Imagine ability and talents as a beautiful flower. What are the three things flowers need to survive and grow? Simple: soil, sunshine, and water. Your potential is similar. Like a flower ready to bloom, your potential needs three simple elements to grow and bloom into accomplishments. Those three things are as follows:

1) Confidence.
2) Drive.
3) Unwavering persistence.

A combination of those three mental weapons is destined for greatness. They all contain a purpose in the grand scheme of your goals and achievements. Your confidence is essential. You need to believe in your abilities. Throughout history, anyone that did anything magnificent had many people doubt them. They doubted their abilities, dreams, and ideas.

The more successful you get in this life, the more people will want to bring you down. This has been proven countless times. What separates the great ones from the average or mediocre is the fact that great individuals never doubt themselves for long periods of time. We all being human, have moments of self-doubt, but it is short lived and rare for a person of greatness. Confidence is key.

    Drive. What does it mean to have a relentless drive? This is my definition: To have an obsession (at times possibly a considered unhealthy obsession) with accomplishing a goal. Anytime you observe a person of greatness, the drive they carry with them can be seen and felt simply by being in their presence. You must have passion to be successful in anything. If you are not passionate about what you are doing, then you are doing something terribly wrong. When you are passionate about something you love, then it needs to be chased. Once the passion has been found, you must care for its growth like the life a newborn child. You must feed it, nurture it, and do whatever you must to help it grow.

Unwavering persistence. This trait is rather simple. Relentlessness. The mindset of someone that gets knocked down 20 straight times without fail by life, and still has the determination to pick themselves up and push back. That is the approach you must have in making your dreams come true. The mindset of, "this is what I want to accomplish. This is what I want to do. I will do it, and no one is going to tell me otherwise." It is a borderline delusional mindset. It is a sense of stubbornness that cannot be altered by negativity.

If you read these traits and find yourself discouraged because they do not describe you, that is alright! Do not let yourself get down because you are not a finished product. The mindset of an entrepreneur doesn't happen by coincidence. It is formed. Like a muscle that needs to be worked on in order to grow, the same can be said for your drive and entrepreneurial spirit. In the next chapter we will discuss how to grow your mind and add to your skillset constantly as you grow both mentally, and financially.

Your mindset is the start of everything if you want to be a winner. Like Babe Ruth said, "It's hard to be beat a person who never gives up." You can learn absurd amounts of useful information about being great from professional athletes, whether you are a fan of their sport or not. How, you may ask? It is simple. Think for a moment about the amount of training and practice these athletes need to put in each and every day to be able to perform the way they do.

It takes just as much mental strength as it does physical strength. It takes the mental makeup of greatness to keep that kind of self-discipline to stick to your extreme diets and long grueling training schedule. We know this to be true, because we have seen plenty of athletes over the years, in a variety of different sports, loose their discipline and get lazy. This affects their bodies, which then affects their performance. We have seen athletes gain weight and ruin their entire careers or have their careers cut short by not taking proper care of their physical health. Outstanding physical gifts are not enough, if you do not possess the mental makeup and mindset to continue to keep up the hard work and push yourself beyond your limits.

I will use an example in the form of now retired NBA superstar Kobe Bryant of the Los Angeles Lakers. When most people think of Kobe, they think 5 time NBA champion, multiple time all-star, MVP, future hall of famer. Kobe had enormous physical gifts to be sure, but do people really stop to consider the almost inhuman work ethic that he possessed? Many tails can be told that can give examples of this, but I will tell two that always astounded me. The first, is told by fellow NBA players Chris Bosh and Dwayne Wade, who recall from the time they played with Kobe in the 2008 Olympics:

"We're in Las Vegas and we all come down for team breakfast at the start of the whole training camp, and Kobe comes in with ice on his knees and with his trainers and stuff. He's got sweat drenched through his workout gear. And I'm like, 'It's 8 O clock in the morning, man. Where in the hell is he coming from? Everybody else just woke up... We're all yawing, and he's already three hours and a full body workout into his day."

The second story is regarding a trainer named Rob who worked with Kobe in the summer of 2012 again for USA Olympic basketball. It starts with Rob giving his phone number to Kobe and telling him to call him anytime to train during his time playing with USA basketball. Two days go by, and Rob wakes up to a call from Kobe at 4:15am:
"Hey, uhh Rob, I hope I'm not disturbing anything right?" said Kobe.
"Uhh no, what's up Kobe?" replied Rob.
"Just wondering if you could just help me out with some conditioning work, that's all." Said Kobe.
Rob answered, "Yeah sure, I'll see you in the facility in a bit."

When Rob got himself out of bed and over to the gymnasium 20 minutes later, he was shocked to find Kobe all alone, covered from head to toe in sweat. Rob recalled that they worked on some conditioning for around 75 minutes. Then they went to the weight room for 45 minutes. Once 7 am rolled around, Rob went back to his hotel to rest. Kobe stayed behind to practice his shooting. Rob came back to the gym around 11 am, exhausted, to find the rest of the players had arrived and were talking to their coach. Kobe was on the other side of the court shooting by himself.

Rob approached Kobe and simply said, "Good work this morning."

"Huh?" replied Kobe.

"Like the conditioning. Good work." Rob stated.

"Oh. Yeah, thanks Rob. I really appreciate it." Kobe answered.

"So when did you finish?" asked Rob.

"Finish what?" Kobe replied.

"Getting your shots up. What time did you leave the facility?" Rob asked.

"Oh just now. I wanted to 800 makes… so yeah, just now." Kobe answered.

Rob was shocked. This was all before the team had even started practice. Are you starting to get the picture? When you are passionate about something, you will do whatever it takes to be great at it. This does not just apply to sports and lifting weights. It can be applied towards anything in life. If you want to be a great public speaker, then practice your speaking until you drop. Practice, until you nail it. If you desire to be a great salesperson, then put the time in and study the art of selling. Put countless hours' in studying and learning every technique. Something like selling is an art form, and like any art form, it must be mastered before you can call yourself an artist.

To acquire greatness, you have to have that fire in your belly, at least a little bit. Whatever you personally need to motivate you, whether it's someone criticizing you, or even if it's hitting a certain goal you have set for yourself, use that to your advantage. All great people are self-motivated. They do not need others to motivate them. This is something that you can develop as long as you are willing to train your mind. Greatness is taking the smallest, most insignificant thing, and making it a mountain in your own mind, and you have to do everything in your power to climb to the top and defeat that mountain.

CHAPTER 8
PERSONAL DEVELOPMENT

The Largest American Lie

Learn the Truth

Jim Rohn (who we discussed earlier in chapter 6), was famous for saying things like, "Don't wish it was easier, wish you were better. Don't wish for less problems, wish for more skills. Don't wish for less challenge, wish for more wisdom.", as well as, "Formal education will make you a living; self-education will make you a fortune.". What on earth does that mean? It is an easily grasped concept, it is the term called personal development. Personal development is what you put into your head. It's self-education to assist you to grow.

As I stated earlier, we as humans are like sponges, meaning that we soak up everything around us. This includes the books you read, the movies you watch, and the people you spend your time with. Take a moment to ask yourself, how are the things I surround myself with most influencing my goals and dreams? If your answer is, perfectly, then you can simply skip this chapter.

If you want a life, larger than that of the average person, then it makes all the sense in the world to develop yourself into an above average person. For most of us, we cannot do this on our own. You can find growth in becoming a reader. The average American, reads one book a year, while many others can go multiple years without picking up a book. I believe this may go hand and hand with the fall of our economy. Now, I am not talking about reading just anything. Reading Harry Potter, or The Hunger Games, may entertain you, but chances are they are not going to grow your mind or better equip you to tackle your dreams.

Wisdom can be found in the mind of those that have already become successful. What if I told you, that wisdom is out in the open, available for anyone and everyone to take it? You might ask, "Where do I sign?". What many do not realize, is that this information is up for grabs in the form of books. Books that help you grow your financial education, spiritual health, ability to keep yourself inspired etc., are priceless. If you wish to grow your skills, then spend time each and every day learning new skills in the form of daily reading.

    The more skills you master, the more valuable you become to the market of your choosing. More value, means more profits. Any amount of money that you can conceive in your mind, the market place WILL pay to a single person.... as long as that person brings enough value to the market place. Is it possible to be paid one million dollars a year? Yes. Is it possible to be paid one billion dollars a year? You bet it is. As long as that individual brings the value needed to back it up. If you bring twenty million dollars into a company, will that company be willing to pay you ten million of that twenty? You better believe it!

You are paid what you are worth, so increase your worth through continuous growth. The more you are capable of doing, the more you will be rewarded.

The average CEO in America reads 60 books per year. Do you think that is just a strange coincidence? Not a chance! Personal growth is magical, because whatever you wish to become, whatever skills you wish to possess, can be obtained through personal growth. What better way to become a great sales person than to read a top sales trainers book? Put their methods into practice, and the scales have just been slightly tipped in your favor. It is the concept of, "do what one does, and you get what they get". Success is a copycat game. If something works well for someone, simply copy it, add your own flavor to it to match your personality and style, and you are on your way. There is no copyright on using the techniques for your own gain, so take advantage!

Does personal development only come in the form of books? Not at all! It can come in audio form, or you could watch seminars in your free time. They can be extremely educational.

What most of you will say after reading this chapter may sound like, "I don't have time for all of this! I am a busy person!". That may be partially true. You may be a busy person, but you always can find the time to read 10 pages of a book a day. It may require you to get up 10-15 minutes earlier than you normally do, but if your success is important enough to you, you will do it. You will make sacrifices in order to achieve your goals if you want it bad enough, but if you would rather sleep those extra ten minutes in the morning, you will have a hard time being great.

Do you drive to work every day? Most of us do. Invest in some audio versions of some books and listen to them on your way to work and on your way home each day. The impact from simply doing that will be felt. There is always a way. You just need to think outside the box and find it.

In Chapter 4, it was said that self-education will always beat out classroom education. It might be one of the most valuable phrases I have heard in my lifetime. It is essential that you take your self-education very seriously. If you want to be the best of the best, you better work to the extreme in developing yourself into the best. Zig Ziglar once said, "You can't have a million-dollar dream with a minimum wage work ethic.". It is as true with the development of yourself as it is with anything else in life.

    The value you bring to the market place is the biggest asset you will ever have in life. Would you rather that value be worth millions, or pennies? This journey is not a one-day task, or one month, it is a lifelong commitment to excellence. The path to self-growth is something that we never see the end of. Why is that? Simple. Because we never stop growing. We never stop learning. Best of all, we can always be better tomorrow than we were today. It is because of this chase of perfection that we can push ourselves to new levels of excellence that we never thought were possible. In a nutshell, your individual achievements have no ceiling to how high they can go. We all can do as much (or as little), with our lives as we choose.

Reflect on the current path you are on in your life. If where you are headed does not excite you, if it doesn't give you chills of excitement, it may be time to form a new strategy. Life should be a truly magnificent journey. If it isn't, it is never too late to change things up. You have greatness in you. All of us do. It is simply up to you to take the necessary steps to reach your full potential.

A majority of people living in today's world will never have the courage to chase what they want most. I am here to tell you, that you can do anything you put your mind to. Life is meant to be outstanding. You deserve to have whatever it is you desire out of life. Don't waste precious time and energy trying to convince your friends and family of what you deserve out of life. Put that effort towards convincing yourself, and what you will have will be endless.

CHAPTER 9
MAKE A PLAN

The Largest American Lie

Learn the Truth

You have successfully discovered what you want to accomplish. Now it is time to make a plan on how to get there. The first step is setting high goals for yourself. If you are a car salesman, take a moment to write out on paper how many cars you want to sell in the next 30 days. I enjoy using sales as an example because every sales activity can be achieved by crunching numbers. In your plan, calculate what is your ratio of deals you normally close. How many cars do you normally sell out of every 10 people you pitch to? If it is 2, then match this with your goal.

If you wish to sell 20 cars in a month, simply do the math on how many people you will need to talk to this month to achieve your goal. Goals can be put into context by doing the math. If you close 2 out of every 10, and you wish to sell 20, then you will need to pitch to 200 people in that given month. Now that you have the expectation of what you need to do, it is time to plan for how you are going to reach those 200 people. This will require you to think outside the box and be creative in your strategy.

    You need to find a way on how to drive more traffic to you. We live in the best time period that has ever existed to accomplish these kind of things. Do research on what draws people to your particular product and begin to advertise. We have tools available to us such as social media, as well as other forms of internet marketing. These are free forms of advertising that can be used at your disposal. Advertise a certain promotion for the next 30 days. Use tactics such as drawings for prizes for everyone that comes to get a free consultation for your particular product or service. Whatever you can think of to get people in front of you.

Do not be afraid to ask your customers for referrals. When you are marketing a certain product, there is no better way to get good quality customers than your current customers' friends and family that see what a phenomenal job you did the first time. People are more open to the idea of buying something if they see someone else they personally know enjoying what they acquired from you. Keep this is mind - we live in a world of envy. If people see someone getting great use out of something that they do not have, they will create the desire to have it themselves, even if it is something they would not have desired on their own. Make sure you are taking care of all of your customers to the best of your abilities, and you will have an easier time getting good recommendations.

If your particular product or service can be marketed by contacting prospects through the telephone, then calculate how many phone calls must be made to hit your certain goal. We live in a day and age where close to all people are walking around with a phone in their pocket.

There are more phones in this country than there are people, so the telephone can be a powerful tool.

    Do not be afraid to link arms with other businesses who provide different products or services than you do. Many businesses know the power of networking, so if you are willing to send your customers to them, chances are they will be more than glad to do the same thing for you in exchange. This goes back to the powerful tactic of obtaining referrals. People do not know who you are, but they are likely more willing to do business with you if you are positively recommended by someone else they either know, or has treated them favorably in the past for a different service.

    Regardless of what type of business you are involved in, writing out how you plan to achieve your goals is an absolute must. A solid game plan must be carried out through equally solid planning.

    Once you have begun to accumulate minor success in your particular field, do not be afraid to invest in your business. Taking risks in business normally is not a bad idea. If you do not believe enough in what you are doing to invest into it, it will say more about your business than it says about the investment. It is important that you believe wholeheartedly in what you are offering to people. If you don't, it may be time to look in the mirror and question if you are marketing the correct product, or possibly may be in the wrong line of work.

Every business comes to a point where an investment in your business is required if you wish for your business to reach the next level. It is better to take the chance and try to stretch your success as far as you possibly can than hold back and always wonder, "what if?".

If you are a telemarketer, and you have decided on your goals of production, calculate how many phone calls need to be made in order to hit your goals. If the number is too large for you to accomplish on your own, seek help. It may not be a bad idea to employ someone to call alongside of you. Two people can reach twice as many people as one. This as well can be looked at as an investment into your business.

It is important to keep an open mind. A closed off mind can easily put a cap on your business success. If you have reached the maximum amount of income that can be earned in your current situation, begin working on a side project. We live in an age where the more streams of income that can be had, the better!

A good example of this is Steve Jobs. In the late 80s and early 90s, shortly after Jobs was pushed out of the company that he founded, Apple computer, he proceeded to create another technology company called NEXT.

For most people, one successful company would have been enough, but Steve Jobs was a special individual for a reason. In 1986, Steve was a large funder for a graphics group that later became Pixar. It took some time, but in 1995 the company released its first film, called Toy Story. The film was the first of its kind and quickly became a blockbuster hit. The gamble paid off big time for Jobs, who became a billionaire in the process.

If you have a successful fast food chain, and have reached a ceiling for financial profit, proceed to open up a second location. Two locations can pull in twice as much revenue as one.

If you are able to, continue to expand your business. If your particular business can no longer be expanded, invest in a second. A great person of interest that we can all learn from on this subject is Warren Buffet.

If at first you do not succeed, continue to learn. The best way to find a formula that works, is to try one that does not a few times first. No one is a failure unless they give up. Great entrepreneurs do not fail. They either succeed, or they learn from their mistakes and become better for it.

A great example of this is Donald Trump. Today, Trump is one of the most recognizable individuals in the world. Since he began to run for presidency, people either love the Donald, or hate him. Regardless of how you feel about him, we all can learn from him in a business aspect. Trump has filed for bankruptcy on four different occasions in his career as a businessman. He is a shining example of perseverance, as today he worth billions of dollars and is one of the most well know personalities not only in America, but on the entire planet.

    Remember to always improve your techniques and do nothing but learn from your short comings. Do not let them defeat you. The only person who can label you as a failure is you, if you give up and admit defeat.

"I have not failed. I've just found 10,000 ways that won't work." -Thomas A Edison.

CHAPTER 10
THE DIFFERENCE BETWEEN OPEN MINDED AND GULLIBLE

The Largest American Lie

Learn the Truth

A good entrepreneur, always keeps his/her mind open to possibilities. Being closed minded can cost you a fortune in the business world. For most of us, it starts with the process of humility. You must humble yourself, put your ego aside, and admit that you don't know everything. In the case of a majority of people, that is one of the most difficult pills to swallow and is a likely reason why many people will read this book and assume they know enough already.

Being closed minded is the reason so many people travel down the traditional path. Once something becomes embedded into our culture, it is difficult to convince someone otherwise. It all has to do with the concept of following the crowd. A majority of college students choose to go to college simply because their parents, friends, or even society tells them to.

    A recent study done in 2013 showed that 75% of college graduates between the ages of 22-32, wished they had received some type of education on financial aid in high school. The study continued to show that a large majority of that 75% stated that they would have highly considered other options if they were aware of what awaited them in college. For most of those college graduates, they probably didn't have too many of their loved ones encouraging them not to go to college. They figured that since everyone around them was proceeding in that direction, that it must be the correct way. That is not being open minded. It is the sign of a closed mind that does not properly explore all of their options.

    Many of us are taught in our upbringings, that open mindedness is a bad trait. If we question our parents, question our teachers in school, or question what we are being preached, we are labeled titles such as, "troublemaker" or "rebel".

Because of this, many children, by the time they reach adulthood, have been programmed that questioning things is wrong, even long into their careers. Keeping the mind open to new possibilities is a foreign concept to far too many people.

There are two concepts that often get confused with one another. The first is being open minded, and the second is being gullible. Despite how often they are confused with one another, they are two very different terms that have completely different meanings.

Let's start with open mindedness. According to the dictionary, it can be defined as follows: "having or showing a mind receptive to new ideas or arguments." Close in on the word receptive. Receptive can be defined as: "having the quality of receiving, taking in, or admitting." Keeping your mind open simply means, you never expel any idea or possibility without doing the proper study to educate yourself on it first. It does not mean to blindly accept any, and all ideas thrown at you with no second thought. Quite the contrary. You keep your options open, and remain open to new ideas regardless of what you think you may know.

Now let us look at what the dictionary definition of gullible is: "easily fooled or cheated; especially: quick to believe something that is not true." When comparing the two words by their meanings, it can easily be deciphered that they are complete opposites from one another. To be gullible is to believe anything you are told, or hear without question. To swallow all that you hear without even knowing if the information is true. An example may be you telling someone that the sky is purple, and them believing you without even so much as looking up.

In many people's minds, the traditional formula preys on the gullible, not the open minded. It wears the hat quite nicely, wouldn't you say? Compare the definition of gullible to how past tradition was explained to you throughout this book and you may see a correlation. Ponder it in your mind. Easily fooled or cheated. I imagine the 75% of college graduates in that study certainly felt fooled and cheated.

Keeping an open mind is seeing an opportunity right in front of you and taking it. Robert Kiyosaki, a bestselling author and well respected entrepreneur, regularly states that people who are poor can be defined as: "Passing Over Opportunities Repeatedly." P.O.O.R.

We all have opportunities come into our lives. What separates the successful from the unsuccessful? It's simple. The successful take opportunities that are placed in front of them. It really is that easy. Some of the greatest people throughout history knew the importance of keeping an open mind. Here are a few we can all learn greatly from:

"The measure of intelligence is the ability to change." -Albert Einstein

"A mind is like a parachute. It doesn't work if it is not open." -Frank Zappa

"Despite my firm convictions, I have been always a man who tries to face facts, and to accept the reality of life as new experience and new knowledge unfolds it. I have always kept an open mind, which is necessary to the flexibility, that must go hand in hand with every form of intelligent search for truth." -Malcolm X

"Always keep an open mind, and a compassionate heart." -Phil Jackson

CHAPTER 11
MAXIMIZE YOUR TALENTS
&
OVERCOME FEAR

The Largest American Lie

Learn the Truth

    You are a beautiful person. You have all the potential you need to make your dreams come true. We all are unique and special individuals in our own way. There is no one like you on the entire planet, and that means you contain talents and skills that are unique to you. Every single person has greatness in them, especially you!

    Once you have discovered what you love, and what your passion in life is, you need to take the next step and pursue it with all of your might. That is the part that most people struggle with. The action. Why is that? It is because of something called fear.

    The average person is absolutely terrified to pursue their dreams. But what part are they afraid of? Simply put, most people are afraid of failure. For a lion's share of potential dream builders in the world, the thought of falling on their face and failing at something is one of the most terrifying thoughts that could enter their head. They fear the ridicule of their peers. They fear the potential financial loss. They fear change.

The great business builders and dream chasers throughout our history, did have fear as well. Great entrepreneurs experience fear just like anyone else. Do they fear failure? You better believe they do. Do they fear the loss of money? At times, of course they do. However, another possibility dominates their mind to a larger degree. They fear living their lives with regrets far more than the fear of failure or loss.

We only have one life, and in the grand scheme of things, nothing can be more frightening than reaching the end of your life and wishing you had at least attempted to achieve the things you always dreamed of. Living with regret is more terrifying than all of those other fears.

Unfortunately, many people have a "here and now" type of thinking. They fail to think in the long term and only focus on what could go wrong at that very moment.

    Entrepreneurs picture 5 years from now, or even 20. They have the gift of setting aside the troubles of today for a much larger picture. All things considered, most of the trials and tribulations that seem life shattering today, are pot holes in the road when you look at the big picture. Keep your mind focused on the future, and you will have greater chance of being successful. In a world where nothing matters more than instant gratification, have the attitude of, "what I do today, will benefit me tomorrow". Do not be afraid to fight the good fight today, so that you may be able to reap the benefits of your hard work tomorrow. That is what being a true entrepreneur, mind and body, is all about.

    Once you have conquered your fear, let nothing stand in your way from living your dreams. As I have said, people will mock, scoff, and think less of you for doing so. All it means in the end is that they feel threatened by your courage. They feel intimidated and concerned that you may actually accomplish what you set out to accomplish one day, and they wish they had the spine to pursue their dreams themselves.

    Consider this.... Why would they feel the need to vocalize to you their disapproval, unless it had something to do with their own insecurity? A person that feels comfortable in their own skin, would simply ignore you, and may just think you are crazy in the privacy of their own thoughts. No person in history did anything remarkable without having a few critics along the way. Just remember, it is normal. Many great entrepreneurs feel that if you have no critics, then you are doing something wrong.

    Your potential is as high as you wish for it to be. Push your limits as far as you can and get the most out of life. During your golden years, you will be able to look back on your life and hold your head high for the amazing things that you accomplished and the legacy you left for the world.

If your goal is to retire young and travel the world, then do exactly that. If your goal is to do something that has never been done, then that is what you must do. We all have different dreams, and we all have different paths. The only thing that will determine your success at the end of the day, is how efficiently you carried out and created your dream.

It is important to take the time to self-reflect on what you choose to call your passion in life, but do not drag your feet for too long. Entrepreneurs (especially young ones) can very easily over think even the smallest activity and cause themselves to doubt their path and change that path constantly. Rethinking your path and goals is not an unwise step to take. That being said, do not let the process become drawn out over a long period of time. Start dream chasing, and start doing so as soon as you can. Each day that the sun sets and you have not taken any steps toward making your dreams a reality is a day wasted. I would like to tell you that we have plenty of time, but we simply do not. Take advantage of the time you have and make life incredible.

    We are taught in school that we must follow "the system", and maybe we will be able to retire during our golden years to still enjoy the remainder of our lives.... If we are lucky. The time has come for us as humans, the highest form of creation on this planet, to start realizing our potential. You can live where you want to live, do what you wish to do, and make exactly what you want to make in your lifetime. Believe in your abilities, and take advantage of this gift we call life.

"If you spend too much time thinking about a thing, you'll never get it done." -Bruce Lee

CHAPTER 12
THE LAW OF ASSOCIATION

The Largest American Lie

Learn the Truth

Every true entrepreneur practices what is known as The Law of Association. As discussed earlier in this book, we as humans act as sponges to a certain degree. All the energy and behavior around us, whether it be positive or negative, gets soaked into who we are and how we behave. We are products of our environment. It is the reason why quite often people of similar educations, hobbies, and sometimes even ethnic backgrounds associate in groups together.

Because of this fact, The Law of Association is practiced by a large majority of entrepreneurs to protect their character, which most of them worked very hard to develop. The law states that whoever you spend the most time with in your life, you will become. The 5 people you surround yourself with most often, will determine what kind of person you ultimately become. If you surround yourself with 5 unmotivated people, chances are, you will become the 6th. If you surround yourself with 5 drug addicts, chances are, you will become the 6th over time.

On the other side of the coin, if you surround yourself with 5 business minded individuals all currently chasing their own respective goals and dreams, chances are you will be the 6th dream chaser. Great speakers over the years have suggested that one should have the goal to surround yourself with 5 millionaires, so that by nature, you will become the 6th.

This can be a very valuable or dangerous rule, depending on how you utilize it. Many people who hear of this philosophy are hesitant to apply it to their own lives for fear of offending their friends and family. I am not suggesting that you eradicate all negative people, or people with negative habits from your life. I am however saying that it may help you greatly if you limit the amount of time you spend with those people. It does not mean that you do not care for them. It simply means that you should spend most of your time with individuals who will bring the best out of you, not the other way around.

    Sometimes it is best to move certain people out of your life. Only you can determine what best course of action to take in any given circumstance. Our lives are too short and too valuable to spend it with people who suck the life out of you and affect you in a negative way. We all should be spending our days with friends who inspire us, and encourage us to do great things.

CHAPTER 13
NEVER STOP GROWING

The Largest American Lie

Learn the Truth

    Your self-education should be an ongoing process. Personal growth is one of the few areas of life where we never move on from the student, to the master. Regardless of your age or experience, we as humans are never a finished product. There is always still more for us to learn because we never will be able to know everything. No one ever has, and no one ever will.

    But that is what makes life magical! We get to experience our growth constantly. The excitement of learning new skills. The enthusiasm about being better tomorrow than you were today is a very significant part of life that makes life worth living.

The lessons that you acquire are not, and most likely will not, be taught to you in a classroom. These are areas that you must invest in yourself and implement into your daily life. You will be better for it in every area of life. If you wish to be a better husband or wife to your spouse, it is possible. Work on yourself. If you desire to be smarter is business, it can be done. Work on yourself. If you are living paycheck to paycheck, and want to make more money, it is in your grasp no matter how far away it may seem. Simply work on yourself, and you can learn the necessary tools to acquire anything you desire in your life. You deserve it.

    What do you do once you are on your way to your own personal glory? Share this content with others. The lie, and scam of the traditional formula that has been crammed down our throats all of our lives, can and will be corrected. It is up to us to bring awareness to the fact, that colleges do not guarantee you a career, and for all the monetary investment spent on them, that is a travesty. A large percentage of companies in our country no longer show loyalty to their employees like we are all brought up to believe. Is this the fault of the companies? Absolutely not! They are not the ones that promised security, and loyalty.... High schools, and colleges did. The time where schools and universities teach close to nothing about money, and true business needs to come to an end. It is up to the true entrepreneurs to stand up and bring awareness to society.

  The education system is not going to do it anytime soon, and neither will the government. It is up to us, the people, to move away from the traditional system. It is up to us to pass this information along, so that the traditional system, will become a thing of the past.

  The perception of the traditional path, should be that it has the potential to work for some individuals, and for others in certain fields, it is a must. However, it is far from the only way, and a majority of kids, with their lives ahead of them, need another way. The time where college graduates get their first taste of the real world drowning in student loan debt needs to become a thing of the past. It all lies, in education. Help your fellow man find the education that could change the direction of his life for the better. Who knows? Someday he may even thank you.

 I close out with a reminder. You can be whatever you wish to be. You can choose to do whatever you want to do. Never settle for a plain life. Your life should be extravagant and exciting! And you know something? I have a feeling it will be.

CHRISTIAN'S TOP TEN MUST READS FOR THE BRAND NEW ENTREPRENEUR

1. As a Man Thinketh by James Allen
2. How to Win Friends and Influence People by Dale Carnegie
3. Rich Dad Poor Dad by Robert Kiyosaki
4. Think and Grow Rich by Napoleon Hill
5. The Secret by Rhonda Byrne
6. The Richest Man in Babylon by George S Clason
7. See You at the Top by Zig Ziglar
8. The Greatest Salesman in the World by Og Mandino
9. The 10X Rule: The Only Difference Between Success and Failure by Grant Cardone
10. The Art of Exceptional Living by Jim Rohn

FOLLOW CHRISTIAN ON YOUR FAVORITE SOCIAL MEDIA!

 @CBrindle24

 @christianbrindle

 Christian Brindle

 Christian Brindle

 @CBrindle24

 @mr.brindle

ABOUT THE AUTHOR

Christian Brindle is a 23-year-old man who lives in Salt Lake City, Utah with his wife, Stormie. He is, as he calls it, a half breed entrepreneur as he currently works as a self-employed independent insurance agent. He is an experienced marketer, networker, and success coach and is currently in the works of starting up his first privately owned company.

Made in the USA
Charleston, SC
16 June 2016